'His verse is immediate, entertaining, engaged with the
world, and his ear for the c...
Stephen Knight, *Independer*

'Congenial, wise-cracking k
Adam Thorpe, *Observer*

'His poems are amusing and charming — effortlessly winning
over an audience when read out loud — yet essentially serious,
substantial enough to repay reconsidering.'
Jeremy Noel-Tod, *Guardian*

'Of the fresh faces that have enlivened poetry over the last
half-dozen years, none has loomed larger and fresher than
that of Simon Armitage.' Mick Imlah, *Vogue*

'Armitage creates a muscular but elegant language of his own
out of slangy, youthful, up-to-the-minute jargon and the
vernacular of his native northern England. He combines this
with an easily worn erudition, plenty of *nous* and the benefit
of unblinkered experience ... to produce poems of moving
originality.' Peter Reading, *Sunday Times*

'Armitage writes with wit and feeling about experiences and
conditions which poetry often turns its back on.'
Jamie McKendrick, *Independent*

Simon Armitage was born in West Yorkshire in 1963. In 1992
he was winner of one of the first Forward Prizes, and a year
later was the *Sunday Times* Young Writer of the Year. He
works as a freelance writer, broadcaster and playwright, and
has written extensively for radio and television. Previous
titles include *Kid, Book of Matches, The Dead Sea Poems,
CloudCuckooLand and Killing Time.*

The Universal H

SIMON

ff

faber and faber

821.914

First published in 2002
ɑber and Faber Limited
ɑre London WC1N 3AU
ɑtes by Faber and Faber, Inc.,
ɑnd Giroux LLC, New York
ɑst published in 2003

ɑet by Wilm. et Ltd, Wirral
Printed in England by Bookmarque Ltd, Croydon

A CIP record for this book
is available from the British Library

ISBN 0-571-21860-1

2 4 6 8 10 9 7 5 3 1

for Susan Elizabeth
and Emmeline Olivia

Acknowledgements

'The Shout' *Gravesiana, Aldeburgh Poetry Anthology*; 'The Twang', 'The English' *Times Literary Supplement*; 'The Laughing Stock' commissioned by BBC Ratio 4; 'Chainsaw verses the Pampas Grass', 'Assault on the Senses', 'A Nutshell', 'The White-Liners', 'Cactus', 'The Stone Beach' *Poetry Review*; 'The Keep' Marco Nereo Rotelli's *Bunker Poetico* project; 'The Nerve Conduction Studies', 'The Flags of the Nations' *reater*; 'Two Clocks' *Time's Tidings* (Anvil); 'Butterflies' commissioned by BBC (Poetry Proms); 'Incredible' *St Luke's Review* (US); 'The Golden Toddy', 'The Jay, The Hard' *London Review of Books*; 'The Night Watchman' *Atlanta Review* (US); 'A Visit' published to accompany Antony Gormley's *Poles Apart* exhibition, Jablonka Galerie, Koln; 'It Could Be You' *Sunday Times*; 'The Strid', 'Birthday' *PN Review*; 'Working From Home' *Heat* (Australia); 'An Expedition' *Rialto* (a version of 'An Expedition' was first performed in Goldthorpe's Yard as part of Wilson and Wilson's production of *House*); 'The Back Man', 'The Wood for the Trees', 'Salvador' *Arete*; 'Butterflies', 'The Laughing Stock' *Short Fuse Anthology* (US); 'The Summerhouse' *The New Republic* (US); 'All for One' *The New Delta Review* (US); 'The Strand' *The Yale Review* (US).

Contents

THE UNIVERSAL HOME DOCTOR

The Shout

We went out
into the school yard together, me and the boy
whose name and face

I don't remember. We were testing the range
of the human voice:
he had to shout for all he was worth,

I had to raise an arm
from across the divide to signal back
that the sound had carried.

He called from over the park – I lifted an arm.
Out of bounds,
he yelled from the end of the road,

from the foot of the hill,
from beyond the look-out post of Fretwell's Farm –
I lifted an arm.

He left town, went on to be twenty years dead
with a gunshot hole
in the roof of his mouth, in Western Australia.

Boy with the name and face I don't remember,
you can stop shouting now, I can still hear you.

The Short Way Home

Here's something you might want to consider.
If I suddenly hit the brakes at night,
for instance on the road between nowhere
and Scapegoat Hill, or on Saddleworth Moor,
I'm only going to reverse the car
thirty or forty yards, so the cat's eye
staring from the gutter might blink again,
taken in by the headlights on full beam.
You see, these things pop from their sockets
after so long, after so many wheels
hammering over, smashing their heads in.
Would you mind stepping out of the transport
and collecting it? Stay transparent, mind –
one hint of shadow and they vaporise.
Be see-through until you've made hand-contact.
And if you're worried about more traffic
coming steaming around this blind corner,
this accident black-spot where my father
once found a biker dead in his helmet,
then I'll punch that red, triangular switch
on the dashboard, trip the hazard-warning lights,
making the car radioactive with amber.
And once you're back in the passenger side
with the seat belt properly clunked and clicked
and I've geared up into fourth or fifth,
why don't you hand it over, the cat's eye,
thank you, which looks like a bullet in fact,
with no moving parts, just a metal case
and a blunt glass bead up front. Not much *use*,
unless you're the type who wants to sit there

with the curtains drawn, shining a torch
into its iris, looking for Jesus.
During my time, I've happened to notice
how the British Police Force handle a torch –
in the overarm, javelin position,
as do night-watchmen, maybe to option
bringing the rear end down like a truncheon
in one flowing movement, without backlift,
without harming the tender filament.
Bang – the weight of five two-volt batteries.
Whereas our grip on the same implement
would be underarm, as with a poker
or garden hose. Pistols are sometimes known
as side arms, right? I've never possessed one,
but as the years go by you lose the use
of your throwing arm to frozen shoulder,
and some old men can no more throw a ball
than they can levitate or somersault.

So there's the thing with the loose cats' eyes, yes.
True. But also the first snow of winter.
If I go downstairs to grind the coffee
and it's all white-on-white through the window,
the roads baffled with snow, nothing moving,
the great outdoors comatose and dreaming,
likely as not I'll open the front door
and scoop a handful from the windowsill.
You'll be half-asleep as I dollop it
on one of those weightless ice-cream wafers
made from communion bread and brown paper
then serve it upstairs like heaven on toast,
food a millionaire might get a taste for.
You'll throw back the sheets, open the curtains

and see that for once in my life, *I'm right*.
Don't ask me if you should eat the thing, though,
it was more of a concept. I can guess
the calorific value of fresh snow,
but it's those other toxins and poisons,
particulates arising from petrol fumes –
hardly the famous Full English Breakfast.
Let that melt and a pound to a penny
holy water won't be the consequence.
Days like those, I'd like to be motoring
through Christmas-card weather over the hills,
but that means an all-terrain vehicle
and snow-chains, which carve up the surface
and crunch all the pleasure out of the ride.
Better to hold back, wait for a full moon
and one of those planetarium nights,
then turn off the headlights and radio.
It's like driving on the pretty B-roads
above Camberwick Green after closedown.
The police wouldn't think much of it, mind,
they're not really that kind of animal,
not really driving-by-moonlight people,
but you might get away with a caution
by keeping a civil tongue in your head.
Be honest – they're not made from pig iron,
the cops, and no less human than we are
given the same uniform and pay-scale.

Does any of that appeal, or not? Don't
say yes just for the sake of saying yes,
I wouldn't want to get so far down the line
only to find you bored out of your box,
giving me one of those screen-saver looks,

or taking the side of the bed nearest
the fire-escape, planning a midnight flit.

But if that were the extent, if I went
so far each time but no further, could you
settle for as much? Could you live with it?

All for One

Why is it my mind won't leave me alone?
All day it sits on the arm of the chair
plucking grey hairs like thoughts out of my skull,
flicking my ear with a Duralon comb.

Evenings when I need to work, get things done;
nine o'clock, my mind stands with its coat on
in the hall. Sod it. We drive to the pub,
it drinks, so yours truly has to drive home.

I leave at sunrise in the four-wheel drive –
my mind rides shotgun on the running board,
taps on the window of my log-cabin,
wants to find people and go night-clubbing.

Social call – my mind has to tag along.
Hangs off at first, plays it cool, smiles its smile;
next minute – launches into song. Then what?
Only cops off with the belle of the belle

of the ball – that's all. Main man. Life and soul.
Makes hand-shadows on the living-room wall.
Recites *Albert and the Lion*, in French,
stood on its head drinking a yard of ale.

Next morning over paracetamol and toast
my mind weeps crocodile tears of remorse
onto the tablecloth. *Can't we be close?*
I look my mind square in the face and scream:

mind, find your own family and friends to love;
mind, open your own high-interest account;
offer yourself the exploding cigar;
put whoopee-cushions under your own arse.

It's a joke. I flounce out through the front door;
my mind in its slippers and dressing gown
runs to the garden and catches my sleeve,
says what it's said a hundred times before.

From a distance it must look a strange sight:
two men of identical shape, at odds
at first, then joined by an outstretched arm, one
leading the other back to his own home.

The Hard

Here on the Hard, you're welcome to pull up and stay.
There's a flat fee of a quid for parking all day.

And wandering over the dunes, who wouldn't die
for the view: an endless estate of beach, the sea

kept out of the bay by the dam-wall of the sky.
Notice the sign, with details of last year's high tides.

Walk on, drawn to the shipwreck, a mirage of masts
a mile or so out, seemingly true and intact

but scuttled to serve as a target, and fixed on
by eyeballs staring from bird-hides lining the coast.

The vast, weather-washed, cornerless state of our mind
begins on the Hard; the Crown lays claim to the shore

between low tide and dry land, the country of sand,
but the moon is law. Take what you came here to find.

Stranger, the ticket you bought for a pound stays locked
in the car, like a butterfly trapped under glass.

Stamped with the time, it tells us how taken you are,
how carried away by now, how deep and how far.

Chainsaw versus the Pampas Grass

It seemed an unlikely match. All winter unplugged,
grinding its teeth in a plastic sleeve, the chainsaw swung
nose-down from a hook in the darkroom
under the hatch in the floor. When offered the can
it knocked back a quarter-pint of engine oil
and juices ran from its joints and threads,
oozed across the guide-bar and the maker's name,
into the dry links.

From the summerhouse, still holding one last gulp
of last year's heat behind its double doors, and hung
with the weightless wreckage of wasps and flies,
moth-balled in spider's wool . . .
from there, I trailed the day-glo orange power-line
the length of the lawn and the garden path,
fed it out like powder from a keg, then walked
back to the socket and flicked the switch, then walked again
and coupled the saw to the flex – clipped them together.
Then dropped the safety catch and gunned the trigger.

No gearing up or getting to speed, just an instant rage,
the rush of metal lashing out at air, connected to the main.
The chainsaw with its perfect disregard, its mood
to tangle with cloth, or jewellery, or hair.
The chainsaw with its bloody desire, its sweet tooth
for the flesh of the face and the bones underneath,
its grand plan to kick back against nail or knot
and rear up into the brain.
I let it flare, lifted it into the sun

and felt the hundred beats per second drumming in its heart,
and felt the drive-wheel gargle in its throat.

The pampas grass with its ludicrous feathers
and plumes. The pampas grass, taking the warmth and light
from cuttings and bulbs, sunning itself,
stealing the show with its footstools, cushions and tufts
and its twelve-foot spears.
This was the sledgehammer taken to crack the nut.
Probably all that was needed here was a good pull or shove
or a pitchfork to lever it out at its base.
Overkill. I touched the blur of the blade
against the nearmost tip of a reed – it didn't exist.
I dabbed at a stalk that swooned, docked a couple of heads,
dismissed the top third of its canes with a sideways sweep
at shoulder height – this was a game.
I lifted the fringe of undergrowth, carved at the trunk –
plant-juice spat from the pipes and tubes
and dust flew out as I ripped into pockets of dark, secret
    warmth.

To clear a space to work
I raked whatever was severed or felled or torn
towards the dead zone under the outhouse wall, to be fired.
Then cut and raked, cut and raked, till what was left
was a flat stump the size of a manhole cover or barrel lid
that wouldn't be dug with a spade or prized from the earth.
Wanting to finish things off I took up the saw
and drove it vertically downwards into the upper roots,
but the blade became choked with soil or fouled with weeds,
or what was sliced or split somehow closed and mended
    behind,
like cutting at water or air with a knife.

I poured barbecue fluid into the patch
and threw in a match – it flamed for a minute, smoked
for a minute more, and went out. I left it at that.

In the weeks that came new shoots like asparagus tips
sprang up from its nest and by June
it was riding high in its saddle, wearing a new crown.
Corn in Egypt. I looked on
from the upstairs window like the midday moon.

Back below stairs on its hook, the chainsaw seethed.
I left it a year, to work back through its man-made dreams,
to try to forget.
The seamless urge to persist was as far as it got.

The Strid

After tying the knot,
whatever possessed us to make for the Strid?

That crossing point
on the River Wharfe

which famously did
for the boy and his dog;

that tourist trap
where a catchment area comes to a head

in a bottleneck stream
above Bolton Abbey;

you in your dress of double cream,
me done up like a tailor's dummy.

Surely it's more of a lover's leap:
two back-to-back rocks

hydraulically split
by the incompressible sap of the spine;

let it be known
that between two bodies made one

there's more going on
than they'd have us believe.

Whatever possessed us, though?
Was it the pink champagne talking?

Or all for the sake of carrying on,
canoodling out of doors,

the fuck of the century under the stars?
Or the leather-soled shoes

with the man-made uppers,
bought on the never-never,

moulded and stitched
for the purpose of taking us

up and across, over the threshold
of water-cut rock and localised moss

in one giant stride,
bridegroom and bride?

A week goes by,
then the rain delivers:

you, like the death of a swan
in a bed of reeds,

me, like a fish gone wrong
a mile down river;

exhibits X and Y,
matching rings on swollen fingers,

and proof beyond doubt
of married life —

the coroner's voice, proclaiming us
dead to the world, husband and wife.

The Twang

Well it was St George's Day in New York.
They'd dyed the Hudson with cochineal and chalk.
Bulldogs were arse-to-mouth in Central Park.
Mid-town, balloons drifted up, red and white streamers

flowed like plasma and milk. The Mayor on a float on Fifth,
resplendent, sunlight detonating on his pearly suit.
The President followed, doing the Lambeth Walk.
It was an election year on both counts. In the Royal Oak

boiled beef was going for a song. Some Dubliner
played along, came out with cockney rhyming-slang,
told jokes against his own and spoke of cousins twice
    removed
from Islington, which made him one of us.

A paper dragon tripped down Lexington, its tongue
truly forked. Two hands thrust from its open throat:
in the left, a red rose; in the right, a collection box
for the National Trust. I mean the National Front.

The Laughing Stock

October. Post meridian. Seven o'clock. We've had tea.
Chip pans cool on pantry shelves. Now we can lounge
on broken settees, scoff bite-size portions of chocolate and
    fat,
crack open a tinnie or two. Skin up. Channel hop.

We're keeping an ounce of toot in a tin for a rainy day.
We talk about work – which corners we cut. Our dogs
lick at the plates on the floor, snort at the ashtray.
Our children are bored, they'll go in the army.

The news was the usual stuff. Like a fire
the telly stays on all the time and our faces and hands
are tanned with the glare. Sit-coms are *so* funny.
The nights draw in, like someone left a tap running.

We're watching a show: *How the Other Half Live*.
Apparently, even at this late hour of an evening, couples
are just setting out to eat. They're friends of the Queen,
as likely as not, and peasant cuisine is an absolute must,

with the wine of the month. Cutlery waits in position.
On FM stations, dinner-jazz plays through open curtains.

Arse-time. Weight off the spine. The hour of the couch.
Now and again, one of us scrubs up well, crosses
the border, gets so far then opens his cake-hole,
asks for meals by the wrong name, in the wrong order.

Why bother? The dishes can wait; we're washing our hair
in the sink, soaking our feet in a bowl. Our dogs
are a joke, disgusting, coming to sniff and to drink
like animal things at the watering hole.

The Strand

We were two-and-a-half thousand miles west
and still putting miles on the clock, driving
at night, the small wooden towns of the coast
coming up in the rain like cargo adrift
then falling away into dark. The road
followed the swell of the land, riding the waves,
then slowed in a town whose name I forget,
a place picked with a pin and an old map
by pricking the bent finger of Cape Cod.
This time we meant it. This time we'd drawn blood.

Evening darkness. Trespass. Walking blindfold
down a private road to a public beach
to fuck, like an order, lie down and fuck.
If the lighthouse shoots us one of its looks,

so what. Then back to the Anglified room
with its Lloyd-loom chairs, its iron bedstead
like the gasworks gates, its Armitage Shanks,
electric candles and motorised drapes.
We dug out the cork from a bottle of red
with the car key, drank from the neck, then slept
naked and drunk on the four-poster bed
with its woolsack mattress and stage-coach springs.
The fire – a paper-pulp, look-a-like log
in its own, flammable, touch-paper bag –
burnt down as neatly in the polished grate
as it should, made flames without smoke or ash
or heat, and got us to dream the endings

of afternoon films and old, hardback books.
A place like this could go up in a flash.

By day we looked for our octopus print
on the beach, but a high tide had been in
to clean and tidy the bay, to flush out
creases and seams. Houses of wood on stilts,
blasted by years and the flacking of salt,
stood back from the front, held on by their roots.
Rock pools were bleary with seaweed and brine.
We were writing our full names on the beach
with our bare feet when I stood on the bird.
Peeled from the sand, hauled and held by its bill,
its parasol wings swung open and out
in a sprained, unmendable twirl. Stone dead –
the sodden quills, the nerveless, leaden flesh.

This was the turning post, the furthest point.
Here was the archaeopteryx of guilt,
this dinosaur hatched from its fossil shell
to doodle-bug out of Atlantic skies
or strike home riding the push of the tide.
It had to be photographed, weighed and sized,
named and sexed, had to be hoisted and hung
by its sharp, arrowhead skull – like a kill.

Then what? Either I raised it to heaven,
arranged its bones as a constellation,
kept on running under the empty stars
of its eyes, under a snow of feathers.
Or I followed the fixed look on your face
to an unmarked circle of sand from where

we could double back, leave this gannet's corpse
beached between open water and blue sky,
eating into the beach, feeding the sea.

The Straight and Narrow

When the tall and bearded careers advisor
set up his stall and his slide-projector

something clicked. There on the silver screen,
like a photograph of the human soul,

the X-ray plate of the ten-year-old girl
who swallowed a toy. Shadows and shapes,

mercury-tinted lungs and a tin-foil heart,
alloy organs and tubes, but bottom left,

the caught-on-camera lightning strike
of the metal car: like a neon bone,

some classic roadster with an open top
and a man at the wheel in goggles and cap,

motoring on through deep, internal dark.
The clouds opened up; we were leaving the past,

drawn by a star that had risen inside us,
some as astronauts and some as taxi-drivers.

An Expedition

We started in over the Great Artex Shield,
ridge-walls taking the shine from the blades of the sleds,
the half-track finding it tough going indeed.
Permanence, ages thick, caked on to some depth.
All the tinned supplies found to be second rate
and the packet stuff got at by morning dew.
We pushed on through.

We lost time, as predicted, became bemused
in the Plains of Anaglypta, drifted for days in the rafts,
tied up each evening in a new swamp, achingly familiar.
Finally, using the paddles to dig, breaching the bank,
we poured through like blood from a blister.
All were rewarded with chocolate and spiced bread.
We pushed forward, ahead.

And the nights were so dark. A deep, concussive dark,
the sort that we carry ourselves, on the inside, under the skin.
And cold, so that bad dreams froze into rock-hard shapes
that wouldn't be thawed by light. And the noonday sun
was a twenty-watt bulb on a threadbare flex
giving watery shadows eighty or ninety feet long.
We dug in, pushed on.

And after the cold, the heat. We slept in the day,
moved at dusk, traversed the Bulkhead in the blackest hours,
bivouacked under a single star so the drop underneath
was too much void to be taken in. We crossed the Porcelain
    Rim
like soldier ants crossing an aeroplane wing, lost a horse

The Stone Beach

A walk, not more than a mile
along the barricade of land
between the ocean and the grey lagoon.
Six of us, hand in hand,

connected by blood. Underfoot
a billion stones and pebbles –
new potatoes, mint imperials,
the eggs of birds –

each rock more infinitely formed
than anything we own.
Spoilt for choice – which one to throw,
which to pocket and take home.

The present tense, although
some angle of the sun, some slant of light
back-dates us thirty years.
Home-movie. Super 8.

Seaweed in ropes and rags.
The weightless, empty armour
of a crab. A jawbone, bleached
and blasted, manages a smile.

Long-shore-drift,
the ocean sorts and sifts,
giving with this, getting back
with the next.

A sailboat thinks itself
across the bay.
Susan, nursing a thought of her own
unthreads and threads

the middle button of her coat.
Disturbed,
a colony of nesting terns
makes one full circle of the world

then drops.
But the beach, full of itself,
each round of rock
no smaller than a bottle top,

no bigger than a nephew's fist.
One minute more, as Jonathan, three, autistic,
hypnotised by flight and fall,
picks one more shape

and under-arms the last wish of the day –
look, like a stone – into the next wave.

Salvador

He has come this far for the English to see,
arrived by bubble through a twelve-hour dream
of altitude sickness and relative speed, of leg room
and feet, headphone headache, reclining sleep.
Jet-lag slung from the eyes like hammocks at full stretch,
Meflaquin pellets riding shotgun in a blister-pack.
This far south for the English to see, as they say.
The hotel drives towards him up the street,
he turns the keyhole anti-clockwise with the key,
the water spins the plug-hole backwards as it drains.
He counts the track-marks in his upper arm
and those in the buttocks and those in the calves,
the pins and needles of shots and jabs, strains and strands,
spores going wild in the tunnels and tubes of veins,
mushrooming into the brain. A polio spider
abseils the drop from the sink to the bath.
Larium country – this far south to broaden the mind.
Look, learn, rise to the day, throw back the blind:
the blue-green flowers of the meningitis tree,
the two-note singing of the hepatitis bird,
the two-stroke buzz of the tetanus bee.
In a puff of chalk a yellow-fever moth
collides and detonates against the window frame.
Malaria witters and whines in the radio waves.
A warm, diphtherial breeze unsettles the pool.
Three hours behind and two days' growth –
hey you in the mirror, shaving in soap,
brushing your teeth in duty-free rum and mini-bar coke,
you with the look, you with the face – it's me, wake up.

The Wood for the Trees

It was the rainforest, so guess what, it pissed down.
And plant-life was the main point of view and not one

of the Leatherman's twenty blades could handle trust.
Trust in a twisted vine or knot in a tree trunk

as a short cut in bare feet back to a grass hut.
Trust in the gift of a green banana-leaf hat,

in the nous of the cockroach captain of a boat
through improbable land-locked dark, wheeling about

in an inch of slurry, seven days from the coast.
Trust in the line and the shining hook, that each cast

lands on the snout of a dogfish as it barks, sinks
to the lip of a catfish as it sleeps or sulks,

dazzles the rainbow bass draped in its national flag
of celestial globes on green-and-yellow flanks.

Trust in the fact that what we want least is to die.
In the neat symmetrical halves of night and day –

noon as a hob of heat to the crown of the head,
midnight's dark as a kettle of black tar set hard.

Trust in the light coming up as the light went down –
dusk as a campfire quashed with a flask of rain, dawn

as the dimmer-switch bloom of the filament plant.
In the upturned palm of a paddle as a plate,

trust in corn with the taste of gravel as enough,
in third-degree sunburn as a fact, in the myth

of the fish with a nose for the urinary tract
as myth, in the trance of a twelve-foot cayman, tricked

by the candle-bright beam of a four-inch torch.
In chicken bones thrown on bare earth as the true church.

In a thumb-print in blood as proof of a man's word,
the back of hand as a map of the known world.

At the furthest point away I woke one morning
after a night of shape-shifting and things moving

in the undergrowth like the wallpaper faces
of childhood, those monsters and other dark forces

alive in the bedroom curtains. Then I wondered
about home, the long journey backwards, and wandered

down to the stream for a drink. What followed the taste
was a sense of calm – calmness in its raw state

and a quietness almost internally near,
Then distant thoughts were suddenly blindingly clear.

The Golden Toddy

We hunted, swept the planet pole to pole
to capture a glimpse of that rare species.

Through a thermal lens we spotted the shoal,
picked up the trail of nuggety faeces

then tagged the shiniest beast in the pride,
mounted a camera on its gleaming horn,
bolted a microphone into its hide.
A first: toddies aflight, asleep, in spawn ...

After months in the field, the broken yolks
had gilded and glazed the presenter's boots;
the sponsor's lover wore a precious skull
for a brooch, out-glinting the best boy's tooth.

Rank bad form. But the creature itself shone,
perched on the clapper-board, the golden one.

Birthday

Bed. Sheets without sleep, and the first birds.
Dawn at the pace of a yacht.

The first bus, empty, carries its cargo of light
from the depot, like a block of ice.

Dawn when the mind looks out of its nest,
dawn with gold in its teeth.

In the street, a milk-float moves
by throw of a dice,

the mast to the east raises itself
to its full height. Elsewhere

someone's husband touches someone's wife.
One day older the planet weeps.

This is the room
where I found you one night,

bent double, poring over
the *Universal Home Doctor*,

that bible of death, atlas of ill-health:
hand-drawn, colour-coded diagrams of pain,

chromosomal abnormalities explained,
progesterone secretion,

cervical incompetence ...
Susan, for God's sake.

I had to edge towards it,
close the cover with my bare foot.

Dawn when the mind looks out of its nest.
Dawn with gold in its teeth.

From the window I watch
Anubis, upright in black gloves

making a sweep of the earth
under the nameless tree,

pushing through shrubs,
checking the bin for bones or meat

then leaving with a backward glance, in his own time,
crossing the lawn and closing the gate.

The Flags of the Nations

The law requires that it is essential to use the correct coloured bag at all times.

White Nylon with
Orange Band:
ALL PATIENTS' PERSONAL SOILED
(dirty) CLOTHING.

White Nylon:
ALL SOILED (dirty) laundry and net bags.

Clear Plastic:
Laundry FOULED with faecal matter, blood, bile, vomit or pus. Fouled items should be placed in a clear plastic bag, and then into a white nylon outer bag.

Clear Water-Soluble:
INFESTED (body lice and fleas).

Red Water-Soluble:
INFECTED laundry, if soiled, from patients with or suspected of suffering from Hepatitis A or B, Typhoid, Paratyphoid, Salmonella, Shigella, Cholera, Anthrax, Poliomyelitis, Diphtheria & HIV.

All such infested/infected laundry should be placed into the appropriate water-soluble bag and then sealed in an outer bag.

Green Plastic:
THEATRE linen only.

Yellow Plastic: Clinical waste for incineration.

Black Plastic: Non-infected household-type waste
                    only. Papers. Flowers.

Splinter

Was it a fall in pressure or some upward force
that went to the head of that spikelet of glass
and drew it through flesh, caused it to show its face
so many years to the day after the great crash.

The Night-Watchman

Waking in cold sweat, he thought of the miller
dunking his head in his day's work
to guard against theft from his precious flour,
sealing every grain and ground in place
with the look in his eye and the twist of his mouth.

Even a finger, licked and dabbed for a taste
would leave a print, a trace. Then thought

of the deep-sea diver or astronaut, home at last,
who peeled the bedspread from his bed and caught
a strange impression in the cotton sheet,
a new expression buried in the pillow-case
beside his wife, and stood

a lifelong minute on the ocean-floor of outer space,
lead-limbed, ashen-faced.

A Visit

for AG

When I opened the door of the cage, the first had flown
from the rig of a pommel horse or the parallel bars
and had come to land on its feet, staking a claim
for a perfect score or a round of applause.
The second had walked the plank, or was poised
on the quivering lip of a diving board, ready to launch
and meet whatever elements might break its fall.
Across an empty room they aped each other, like for like,
and were cast as twins, but even to me it was plain enough
that one was a touching down to the other's taking off.
I paced out seven equal strides in leather boots
between the two, then killed some time in the gap,
the space which was also a force, a for and against
that kept them close and held them apart, and I sensed
a balancing act of sorts, a line to be crossed.
They were taller than me by as much as a hand,
and in sizing them up they followed suit, pressed back
against their metal frames to show off finer points:
the A-shape where the collar housed the neck,
the apple in the throat, like a clot, like an egg,
lips that were sealed with a smear of flux,
the seam – some International Date Line running crosswise
to the scalp, the cockpit of the frontal lobes,
the death-mask and the life-mask, facing up, exchanging looks.
True, side on they were ordinary men in the nude.
But fore and aft they lifted their wings to a height
that covered the join where solid earth meets open sky,
and one couldn't shield the world from the world's dark,
and one couldn't stoop or hunch to let in the light,

but they carried their weight, shoulder to wrist
with arms assumed into the leading edge of flight.
Thumped with a fist, they rang with a depth
of a church bell or cargo door slammed shut, and dust
was sunburnt skin, the orange-brown psoriasis of rust.
Within, one form held firm against the audience of air.
Without, one form encased the bubble of its heart.

In distant rooms came the circus of family and friends:
blotted faces leering out of picture frames; the man
who slept too long on his bed of nails, and turned
in the night, and rose at dawn in an aura of thorns,
pegs instead of body hairs, spikes which were thoughts.
And pipe-cleaner man with his igneous bones, pigeon-toed,
some cousin of the ploughshare and the tuning fork.

But the angels of iron, they were the things: flying machines
dreamed up, pilots and 'planes in the same breath.
Consider these works. Stand, dumb-struck in the field,
between the poles. Take in those forms: this earth-piece
bolted by its presence to a starting block;
this lectern, gliding by the metal pages of a book.

The Jay

I was pegging out your lime-green dress;
you were hoping the last of the sun
might sip the last few beads of drip-dry water
from its lime-green hem.

I had a blister-stigmata the size of an eye
in the palm of my hand
from twisting the point of a screw
into the meat of the house. Those days. Those times.

The baby bird was crossing the gravel path
in the style of a rowing boat crossing dry land.
Struck with terror when I held it tight
in the gardening gloves of humankind, we saw for ourselves

the mouse-fur face and black moustache,
the squab of breast-meat under its throat,
the buff-brown coat and blue lapels,
the painted inside of its mouth,

the raw, umbilical flute of its tongue
sucking hard at the sky for a taste of air.
Setting it free, it managed no more than a butterfly stroke
to the shade of an evergreen tree, where we let it be.

They say now that the basis of life
in the form of essential carbon deposits
could have fallen to earth as a meteorite, or comet,
and that lightning strikes from banks of static

delivered the spark that set life spinning.
But this three-letter bird was death, death thrown in from
  above,
death as a crash-brained, bone-smashed, cross-feathered
  bullet,
so we could neither kill it nor love it.

The Nerve Conduction Studies

We ask that watches and rings are removed.
We ask that trousers are rolled to the knees,
sleeves to the elbow. We ask for clean feet,
any wounds to be dressed, hands to be warmed

in the sink to bring blood close to the skin.
Would sir say sir was sensitive to pain?
Cold metal on bare flesh comes as a shock.
We loop conductive strips over the toes

and fingers, press conductive strips and pads
into the calves and wrists, and we ask
that electrolyte dripping from elbows
and heels not be mistaken for cold sweat.

We ask that questions of voltage are saved
till last; diabetics, for some reason,
feel less – we crank up the current, sometimes
forget, but in layman's terms we can state

that a small charge makes a tour of the nerves
by way of the brain. We measure the speed.
There, like the graph of the song of the whale
the trace comes up on the screen and we ask

for a second or third flick of the switch
if the jolt doesn't travel the distance
the first time. All in the head, is it not?
They say it's relative, but they don't say

to what. We ask that a pillow be placed
in the lap; we advise eyes to the front.
Humour is good – a good chance for a joke,
that it wouldn't take much to make sir talk

but a mind with nothing to hide or fight
is amazingly weak. In point of fact,
men with hard, dark faces are tickled pink.
Elderly women hardly even flinch.

We offer sweet tea in a plastic cup
and point to the door with a fountain pen.
Before starting up, unwind in the car:
let the sickness pass, let the windscreen clear.

Findings are by post except in the case
of freak results or a rare disorder.
These tests are well known to hold true; we trust
they prove nothing less than you dared hope for.

The White-Liners

They do the white line.
It's tough going, hard on the body, life on the road.
You find them everywhere: motorways, high streets, English
   country lanes.
They've done thousands of miles, leaving their trails behind.

They operate in traffic, sometimes at night.
Blind corners and accident black-spots are part of the job.
Their dreams are chevrons, zebras, pelicans and cats' eyes.
They eke out their stuff, cut it with all kinds of crud.

You'd think they could tell a few tales – you'd be wrong.
It's the classic case, the original one-track mind.
Years go by like cars, landscapes rise and fall
in front of their eyes, but the song is the same:

white lines, how they're the white-liners, doing the white line.

The Summerhouse

With the right tools it was less than a day's work.
It wasn't our trade, but a wire-brush was the thing
for fettling mould and moss from bevelled window frames.
Sandpaper took back old wood to its true grain.

Winter pressed its handshake, even through thick gloves.
From the boozy warmth of the boiler-room I lugged
a litre tin of Weatherseal, and popped the lid.
Strange brew. Varnish or paint? Water-based, it had a tone

or shade, but carried solvent on its breath
and held the stars and planets of a pinhole universe
suspended in its depth. Some gemstone in its liquid state –
it fumed when ruffled with a garden cane.

Winter stood on the toe-end of leather boots.
And as the substance in the tin went down it lost its shine
and from its lower reaches came a sluggishness –
a thick, begrudging treacle, and the colour brown.

Some change in temperature was the root cause.
Rifles stamped their feet and clapped their hands together
over on the firing-range. It was going dark
but unconcerned we dipped the brushes for a second coat.

It was time-travel, of a sort. Having given our all
to this chapel of sun-loungers and soft drinks,
to the obvious glory of ultraviolet light, we found ourselves
standing instead by a wooden shed, painted with mud and shit.

Butterflies

Is it astral alignment or plain old quirk of fate
that the road over the knoll takes a shot at the moon
or reaches out for the sun, like one of those phantom limbs
still alive and well in the minds of amputees?

Don't stop, there's nothing there. No marker stone,
no weather station locked in a white hut, no seat
for the view, no clockwork stereoscope with both eyes shut
and a slot for old money, jammed with a lolly stick.

Instead, just drive – it's a stepping off into the unknown.
Kids in the back of the car would sing out to take it at speed,
    release
the stomach's lepidoptera – red admiral and cabbage white –
like a million in used notes, swept up by a freak wind.

Even at our age and alone, some instinct in the toes or heel
wants to let rip over the brow of that hill, let body and soul
divide, the heart in its seat-belt, hands locked on the wheel
but the spirit propelled through the windscreen – weightless,
    thrown . . .

True, people we know have gone up and never come down.
Timing is all it takes, some biker or driver at full pelt,
thinking the same thing, coming the other way. But in our
    world,
that's how these creatures form, how the wings are made.

The English

They are a gentleman farmer, living
on reduced means, a cricketer's widow
sowing a kitchen garden with sweet peas.
A lighthouse-keeper counting aeroplanes.

Old blackout curtains staunch the break of day.
Regard the way they dwell, the harking back:
how the women at home went soldiering on
with pillows for husbands, fingers for sons,

how man after man emerged at dawn
from his house, in his socks, then laced his boots
on the step, locked up, then steadied himself
to post a key back through the letterbox.

The afternoon naps, the quaint hours they keep.
But since you ask them, that is how they sleep.

It Could Be You

We interrupt our live coverage of the War
for details of tonight's National Lottery draw:

the winning numbers are fourteen, eighteen,
thirty-nine, forty-four, eighty-two, and ninety-one.

The bonus ball is number two-thousand-and-some.
A record jackpot pay-out will be shared between

winning ticket holders in Belfast, Aberdeen,
Milford Haven and East Acton. Now back to the action.

A Nutshell

It's too easy to mouth off, say
how this matchwood-and-cotton ship of the line
got where it is today,

how it put into port,
shouldered home through the narrow neck
of a seamless, polished-off ten-year-old malt,

came to be docked
in a fish-eye, bell-jar, wide-angle bottle
shipshape and Bristol fashion.

See, the whole thing was rigged
and righted itself at the tug of a string
or turn of a screw, main mast raised

to its full height,
every detail correctly gauged, taffrail
to figurehead, a model of form

and scale right down
to the glow of coal and the captain,
toasting himself in the great cabin.

It's the same kind of loose talk
that cost us dear, put fire in the chimney breast,
smoking the stork from its nest.

At the end of the day couldn't we meet
half-way, in an autumn field
in the stubble of hay,

hearing the chink, chink, chink
of cheers, prost, mud in your eye, and stumble
through gate or arch

to emerge on an apple orchard
in full cry, where tree after tree bends double
with glass, where every growth

blows a bubble or flask of fruit-in-the-bottle –
Jupiter, James Grieve, Ashmeads Kernel –
branch after branch of bottled fruit,

there for the picking, preserved in light?

Working from Home

When the tree-cutter came with his pint-size mate,
I sat in the house but couldn't think.
For an hour he lurked in the undergrowth,
trimming the lower limbs, exposing the trunks.

I moved upstairs but there he was, countersunk eyes
and as bald as a spoon, emergent in orange rays,
head popping out through leafage or fir,
a fairy light in the tree of heaven,

a marker-buoy in the new plantation of silver pine.
Or traversing, bough to bough, from one dead elm
to the next, or holding on by his legs only
or accrobranching the canopy. At lunch,

he pulled the wooden ladder up behind,
perched in the crown of a laurel, and smoked.
He nursed the petrol-driven chainsaw like a false arm.
The dwarf swept berries and beech-nuts into a cloth bag.

I was dodging between rooms now, hiding from view.
Down below they cranked up the chipping machine,
fed timber and brushwood into the hopper.
Through a gap in the curtains I looked, saw into its maw –

steel teeth crunching fishbone twigs,
chomping thick wood, gagging on lumber and stumps.
Sawdust rained into the caged truck.
Birds were flying into the arms of a scarecrow

on the Pole Moor, or leaving for Spain. I sat on the steps
between ground-floor and upstairs, thought of his face
at the bathroom window watching me shave,
his lips in the letterbox, wanting to speak.

Assault on the Senses

In the Line of Sight
mixed media:
carousel projection of assassinated world leaders viewed through telescopic sight consisting of spent bullet-casing and cross-hairs formed by two of artist's own eyelashes. Private collection.

What I Feel I Can't Touch, What I Touch I Can't Feel
mixed media/working model:
two coin-operated mechanical fun-fair 'cranes' in glass case, right claw wearing full-size boxing-glove, left claw wearing yellow washing-up glove, both suspended above one-hundred assorted family photographs belonging to artist, face up. One old penny per go. Private collection.

By Any Other Name
mixed media/working model:
cross-section of human head (nose-part moulded from artist's own sun-dried mucus) nasally exhaling carbon monoxide fumes generated by miniature petrol-driven engine housed within alabaster brain-cavity. Foregrounded by red rose wearing face-mask. Private collection.

Sweet Tooth
mixed media:
moulded impression of artist's own mouth, gums cast in boiled sugar, teeth sculpted from Kendal Mint Cake. Private collection.

Timing How Long I Can Stand a Loud Noise before Giving In
looped video presentation:
black-and-white film of artist in recording studio positioned
between two in-turned loud-speakers broadcasting increasing
volume of feedback. Foregrounded by graphic equaliser and
stopwatch. Private collection.

Walking on the Moon
colour photograph on teflon-coated aluminium:
self-portrait of artist's own toes painted as ten astronauts
with toe-nails as helmet visors, set against computer-
enhanced image of deep space. Private collection.

Music to the Ears
mixed media:
wall-mounted treble and bass clef fashioned from artist's
own ear-wax, vacuum-packed in transparent polythene.
Private collection.

Shit for Brains
mixed media:
glass case containing baked life-size brain sculpted in artist's
own excrement, positioned on domestic 'Libra' weighing
scales, overbalanced by tin of dog meat. Private collection.

Samson and Vagina
mixed media:
'Samsonite' model of female crotch contorted into facial
mask, wearing wig constructed from artist's own head of
hair grown to shoulder-length over several years. Private
collection.

Blood, Sweat and Tears
two framed pictures:
lettering and numbering of chemical equation for oil and
chemical equation for canvas, painted in solution of artist's
own blood, sweat and tears on tenterhooked rectangle of ar-
tist's epidermis. Private collection.

ii) REGISTER

The Gallery would like to recognise the inestimable con-
tributions made by or on behalf of the following, without
whom *Assault on the Senses* would not have been possible:

>   Gargantuan Interests Ltd
>   Raymond Kunt III
>   International Contaminates
>   Dr Malcolm Armsrace, OBE
>   The Gotten Family
>   Blabbermouth Promotions
>   The Gross Foundation
>   UltraBulk Foodstuffs
>   Sir Paul Oilfield
>   Mr Donald Tribeslayer, Jnr
>   The Capital Hospital for the Hopelessly Incurable plc

The Gallery also extends its acknowledgements to the great
number of unlisted associates whose involvement gave shape
and meaning to this exhibition.

Cactus

I'm putting all my hurt in one carrier-bag
and slinging the lot.
A sensitive tooth
that cowers from coffee and cold drinks;

a size-ten headache – drink-related – from last night,
worn like a crown
on the head of a child prince;
pins and needles, at it

like blackfly in the fingertips;
a shoulder-joint with metal fatigue;
stitch if I over-stretch or run;
grandmother's blessings peeling from both thumbs.

The barium meal of intense, personal hate.
Bad reviews for a good book –
dog turds on the lawn at first light.
My aching back.

The apostle spoon
of walking out and leaving a note;
the Maundy money
of things unsaid;

old photographs, dry bread.
The boomerang of a death
not happened, not yet.
That's about it.

Carting it down to the tip
I sense it coming together as one mass,
all its solids and slop
making a single, stubborn piece.

Splinters like wooden toothpicks
puncture the bag.
Peeling the plastic back I find
a cactus rooted in an iron pot –

rubbery flesh,
limbs like the limbs of a doll.
Its spikes stab the air
guarding sun-spot, jelly-tot buds

bearded with yellow fur.
So now I'm torn:
with its loveable form,
plausible fruits and cocktail sticks

it's a dangerous thing.
But tagged with its common name,
draped with a ribbon and sent to the right address,
actually it's a great gift.

Two Clocks

In the same bedroom we kept two small clocks,
one you could set your watch by, the other

you could not. The night we lost the good clock
under the bed the other seemed to know

to take its turn and was a metronome
until the lost clock was found. Then it stopped.

Like emergency lighting kicking in
during a power-cut, or biking it

half-asleep on the back of a tandem,
or gliding home with the engine broken.

And since neither of us can talk freely
on Albert Einstein's General Theory,

electromagnetic flux, black magic
or the paranormal, let us imagine

that all objects and events are open
to any meaning we choose to give them

and that if the absence of one timepiece
causes another to take up the pace

then these clocks could be said to demonstrate
some aspects of our love or private thoughts.

Stretching the point to another level,
maybe the effect is causal, and life —

if we could get things right on a small scale,
between people — might conform to this rule

of like for like; it could be that simple.
Maybe these clocks are a poor example.

The Back Man

Five strong, we were, not including the guide,
five of us walking a well-trodden path
through the reserve, from the camp to the stream
and the flooded forest on the far side.
Dragonflies motored past like fish on the wing.
Beetles lifted their solar-panelled shells.
A bird, invisible, ran through its scale
like a thumbnail strummed on a metal comb.
The branches of trees were shelves in a shop
selling insect brooches and snakeskin belts
and miniature frogs with enamelled heads.
The monkeys fancied themselves as soft toys.
Blue orchids offered themselves without shame.
Late afternoon, and the heat in the shade
was stale and gross, a queasy, airless warmth,
centuries old. I was the last in line,

the back man, when from out of nowhere
it broke, I mean flew at me from behind
and I saw in my mind's eye the carved mask
of its face, the famous robe of black fur,
the pins and amulets of claws and feet,
the crown and necklace of its jaws and teeth
all spearing into the nape of my neck.
I dropped the hunting knife and the shooting stick.

The rest of the group had moved on ahead.
The blades and feathers of grasses and ferns
conducted something in the air, but time
was static, jammed shut. Nerves strained with the sense

of a trap half-sprung, a pin almost pulled
and all noise was a tight thread stretched and thinned
to breaking point and blood in its circuit
awaited a pulse. The turnpike of a branch
bent slowly back to shape across the trail.
Up high, a treetop craned its weather vane;
a storm-cloud split and it started to rain.
I was shouldered home in the fibreglass tomb
of a yellow canoe. Then sat up straight –
alive. Unharmed, in fact. In fact untouched.

I've heard it said that a human face
shaved in the hairs on the back of a head
can stop a jaguar dead in its tracks,
the way a tattoo of Christ, crucified
across the shoulder blades and down the spine,
in past times, could save a thief from the lash.
Years on, nothing has changed. I'm still the man
to be hauled down, ripped apart, but a sharp
backward glance, as it were, is all it takes.
I sense it mostly in the day-to-day:
not handling some rare gem or art object
but flicking hot fat over a bubbling egg,
test-flying a stunt-kite from Blackstone Edge,
not swearing to tell the whole truth on oath
but bending to read the meter with a torch,
tonguing the seamless flux of a gold tooth,
not shaking the hands of serial killers
but dead-heading dogwood with secateurs,
eyeballing blue tits through binoculars,
not crossing the great ocean by pedalo
but moseying forward in the middle lane,
hanging wallpaper flush to the plumb-line,

not barrelling over sky-high waterfalls
but brass-rubbing the hallmarks of fob-watches,
lying on top of sex, in the afterwards,
not metal-detecting the beach for land-mines
but tilting the fins of pinball machines,
pencilling snidey comments in the margins,
not escaping into freedom or peacetime
but trousering readies extruded from cashpoints,
eating the thick air that blasts the escarpment,
not rising to the bait of a fur coat
but yacking on the cordless, cruising Ceefax,
checking the pollen-count and long-range forecast,
not whipping up the mother-of-all soufflés
but picking off clay pipes with an air-rifle
at the side-show, describing myself as
white in the tick-box, dipping the dipstick,
needling pips from half a pomegranate,
not cranking up the system to overload
but licking the Christian Aid envelope,
lining up a family photograph,
not chasing twisters across Oklahoma
but changing a flat tyre on the hard shoulder,
dousing for C4 with a coat hanger,
not carving a slice from the Golden Calf
but hiking the town's municipal golf course,
drowning an inner tube in a horse trough,
not feeling the sonic boom bodily
but swiping a key card in the hotel lobby,
easing up for the lollipop lady,
not inhabiting the divine sepulchre,
not crowing over Arctic adventure,
not standing gob-smacked beneath ancient sculpture,
not kneeling empty-handed, open-mouthed

at the altar, but in the barber's chair
or tattoo parlour, in a sleepy trance,
catching in the mirror the startled face
of some scissor-hand, some needle-finger.

The Keep

Sleep she on the eastern side,
holding a dream intact.

Sleep he turned to the west,
nursing a cracked rib.

Spine to spine, night over
turn they and face, make good

in the bed's trench. None break,
one keep in the bone crib.

Incredible

After the first phase, after the great fall
between floorboards into the room below,
the soft landing, then standing one-inch tall
within the high temple of table legs
or one-inch long inside a matchbox bed ...

And after the well-documented wars:
the tom-cat in its desert camouflage,
the spider in its chariot of limbs,
the sparrow in its single-seater plane ...

After that, a new dominion of scale.
The earthrise of a final, human smile.
The pure inconsequence of nakedness,
the obsolescence of flesh and bone.
Every atom ballooned. Those molecules
that rose as billiard balls went by as moons.
Neutrinos dawned and bloomed, each needle's eye
became the next cathedral door, flung wide.

So yardsticks, like pit-props, buckled and failed.

Lifetimes went past. With the critical mass
of hardly more than the thought of a thought
I kept on, headlong, to vanishing point.
I looked for an end, for some dimension
to hold hard and resist. But I still exist.